This book belongs to

Name: _____

©All rights reserved-Math-Knots LLC., VA-USA

www.math-knots.com

Copy right © 2019 MATH-KNOTS LLC

All rights reserved, no part of this publication may be reproduced, stored in any system or transmitted in any form, or by any means, electronic, mechanical, photocopying, recording, or otherwise without the written permission of MATH-KNOTS LLC.

Cover Design by :
MATH-KNOTS LLC

Second Edition :
December, 2020

Author:
Gowri Vemuri

Questions: mathknots.help@gmail.com

* NNAT® and Naglieri Nonverbal Abilities Test ® are registered trademarks of Riverside Publishing company (A Houghton Mifflin Harcourt company) is neither affiliated, nor sponsors or endorses this product.

Dedication

This book is dedicated to:

My Mom, who is my best critic, guide and supporter.

To what I am today, and what I am going to become tomorrow,

is all because of your blessings, unconditional affection and support.

This book is dedicated to the

strongest women of my life ,

my dearest mom

and

to all those moms in this universe.

G.V.

©All rights reserved-Math-Knots LLC., VA-USA

www.math-knots.com

©All rights reserved-Math-Knots LLC., VA-USA

www.math-knots.com

What is NNAT ?

The Naglieri Nonverbal Ability Test (NNAT) is a group nonverbal ability test. These tests serve as a measure for identifying and placing students of K-12 for gifted and talented or Advanced Academic programs in many schools across USA.

The NNAT test is based on complex geometric shapes and figures to evaluate problem-solving and reasoning abilities of a child.

The test doesn't require mastery of any language, quantitative aptitude and Reading skills and uses minimum directions to solve the questions. The test measures the advanced levels of reasoning abilities of the child.

There are 4 types of questions on the NNAT test:

Pattern completion: Students Identify the missing portion of the given picture.
Reasoning by analogy: Relationship between the abstract geometric shapes is identified
Serial reasoning: A sequence of shapes, objects are identified

Example: the pattern is 1 ,2,3 then next row is
either 3 , 2, 1 or 2, 3, 1 and the third row is 2, 3, 1 or 3 , 2, 1
based on second row choice.
NOTE: NO two rows will have the same pattern

©All rights reserved-Math-Knots LLC., VA-USA www.math-knots.com

What is NNAT ?

Spatial visualization: Two or more objects are combined to form a new object

Level	Grade	Pattern Completion	Analogy	Serial Reasoning	Spatial Visualization	Total
A	K	30	8			38
B	1	19	13	6		38
C	2	10	12	11	5	38
D	3-4	6	10	8	14	38
E	5-6	5	6	8	19	38
F	7-9	2	10	8	18	38
G	10-12		7	7	24	38

©All rights reserved-Math-Knots LLC., VA-USA

www.math-knots.com

Start from the middle of right choice and fully fill the bubble completely.

Wrong

A   B ◯   C ◯   D ◯

Wrong

A ◯   B ◯   C ⊗   D ◯

Wrong

A ◯   B ◯   C   D ◯

Partial Filled Bubble is not correct.

Correct

A ◯   B ◯   C ●   D ◯

©All rights reserved-Math-Knots LLC., VA-USA

www.math-knots.com

PREPARATION FOR THE TEST

1. To simulate the testing format, a parent or an adult shall read the questions to the student to answer the practice test sets.

2. Student need to have a pencil and an eraser.

3. Student need to make sure they are bubbling the circles in the right way.

Before the testing date.

1. Make sure the child has a good nights sleep and a good breakfast.

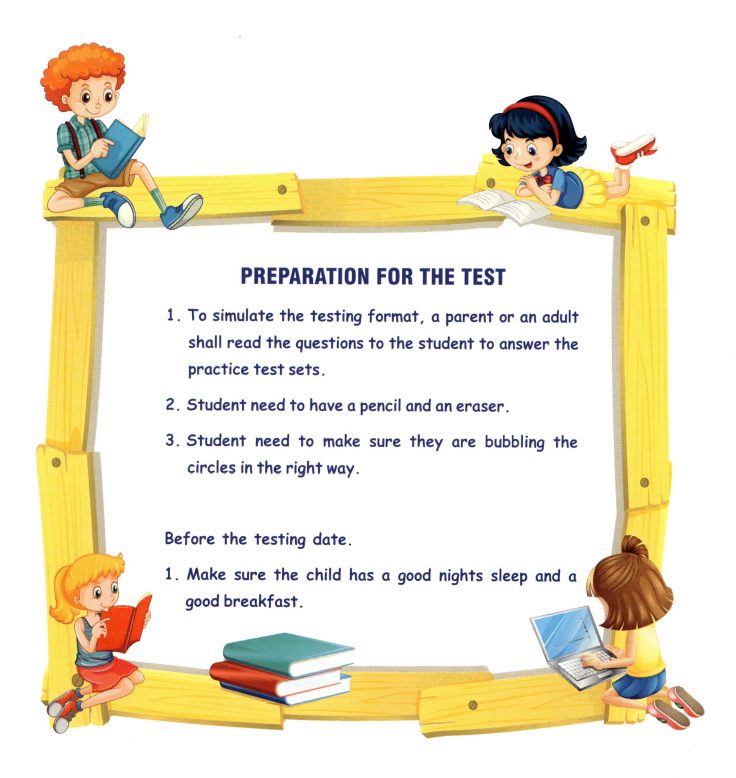

©All rights reserved-Math-Knots LLC., VA-USA

www.math-knots.com

©All rights reserved-Math-Knots LLC., VA-USA

www.math-knots.com

©All rights reserved-Math-Knots LLC., VA-USA

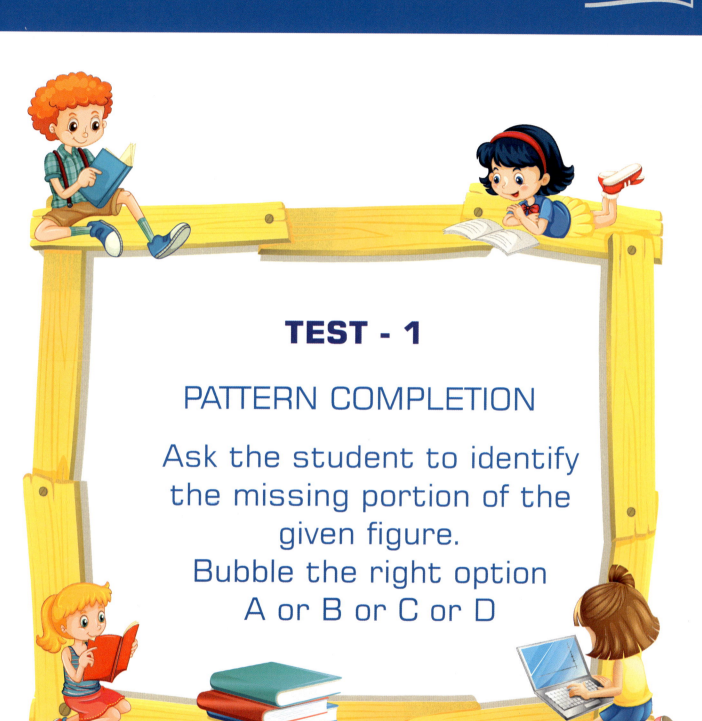

TEST - 1

PATTERN COMPLETION

Ask the student to identify
the missing portion of the
given figure.
Bubble the right option
A or B or C or D

Lets Start the Test...

©All rights reserved-Math-Knots LLC., VA-USA

www.math-knots.com

©All rights reserved-Math-Knots LLC., VA-USA

1)

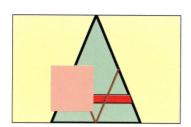

(A) ○

(B) ○

(C) ○

(D) ○

2)

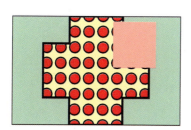

(A) ○

(B) ○

(C) ○

(D) ○

©All rights reserved-Math-Knots LLC., VA-USA
For more practice visit www.a4ace.com

www.math-knots.com

3)

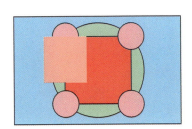

(A) ○   (B)○   (C) ○   (D) ○

4)

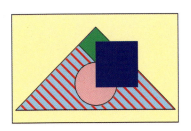

(A) ○   (B)○   (C) ○   (D) ○

©All rights reserved-Math-Knots LLC., VA-USA
For more practice visit www.a4ace.com

www.math-knots.com

5)

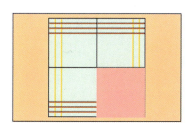

 (A) ○

 (B) ○

 (C) ○

 (D) ○

6)

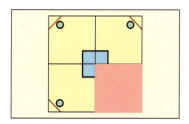

 (A) ○

 (B) ○

 (C) ○

 (D) ○

©All rights reserved-Math-Knots LLC., VA-USA
For more practice visit www.a4ace.com

www.math-knots.com

7)

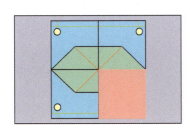

(A) ○   (B) ○   (C) ○   (D) ○

8)

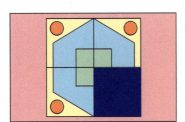

(A) ○   (B) ○   (C) ○   (D) ○

©All rights reserved-Math-Knots LLC., VA-USA
For more practice visit www.a4ace.com

www.math-knots.com

9)

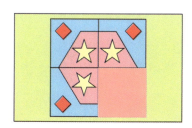

(A)   (B)   (C)   (D)

10)

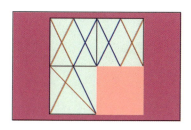

(A) ○   (B)   (C)   (D)

©All rights reserved-Math-Knots LLC., VA-USA
For more practice visit www.a4ace.com

www.math-knots.com

11)

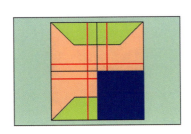

(A) ○

(B) ○

(C) ○

(D) ○

12)

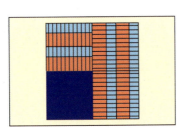

(A) ○

(B) ○

(C) ○

(D) ○

©All rights reserved-Math-Knots LLC., VA-USA
For more practice visit www.a4ace.com

www.math-knots.com

13)

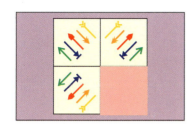

(A) ○

(B) ○

(C) ○

(D) ○

14)

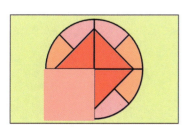

(A) ○

(B) ○

(C) ○

(D) ○

©All rights reserved-Math-Knots LLC., VA-USA
For more practice visit www.a4ace.com

www.math-knots.com

15)

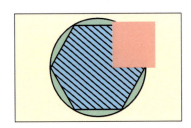

(A) ○

(B) ○

(C) ○

(D) ○

©All rights reserved-Math-Knots LLC., VA-USA
For more practice visit www.a4ace.com

www.math-knots.com

TEST - 1

REASON BY ANALOGY

Ask the student to identify the relationship between the abstract geometric shapes given in the first row based on the same relationship identify the missing figure in the second row.
Bubble the right option
A or B or C or D

Lets Start the Test...

©All rights reserved-Math-Knots LLC., VA-USA

1)

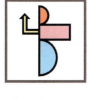

(A) ○   (B) ○   (C) ○   (D) ○

2)

(A) ○   (B) ○   (C) ○   (D) ○

©All rights reserved-Math-Knots LLC., VA-USA

www.math-knots.com

3)

(A) ○   (B) ○   (C) ○   (D) ○

4)

(A) ○   (B) ○   (C) ○   (D) ○

©All rights reserved-Math-Knots LLC., VA-USA
www.math-knots.com

NNAT
Reasoning by Analogy

5)

(A) ○   (B) ○   (C) ○   (D) ○

6)

 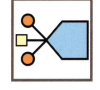

(A) ○   (B) ○   (C) ○   (D) ○

©All rights reserved-Math-Knots LLC., VA-USA

www.math-knots.com

7)

(A) ○   (B) ○   (C) ○   (D) ○

8)

 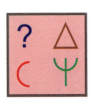

(A) ○   (B) ○   (C) ○   (D) ○

©All rights reserved-Math-Knots LLC., VA-USA

www.math-knots.com

9)

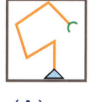

(A) ○   (B) ○   (C) ○   (D) ○

10)

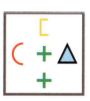

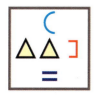

(A) ○   (B) ○   (C) ○   (D) ○

©All rights reserved-Math-Knots LLC., VA-USA

www.math-knots.com

11)

(A) ○　　　(B) ○　　　(C) ○　　　(D) ○

12)

 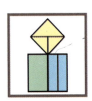

(A) ○　　　(B) ○　　　(C) ○　　　(D) ○

©All rights reserved-Math-Knots LLC., VA-USA

www.math-knots.com

13)

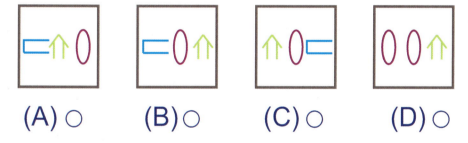

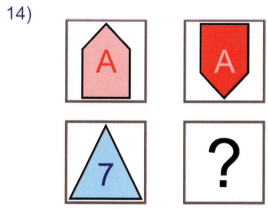

(A) ○   (B) ○   (C) ○   (D) ○

14)

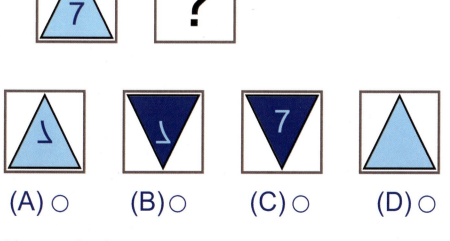

(A) ○   (B) ○   (C) ○   (D) ○

©All rights reserved-Math-Knots LLC., VA-USA

www.math-knots.com

15)

 ?

(A) ○   (B) ○   (C) ○   (D) ○

TEST - 1

SERIAL REASONING

Ask the student to identify the sequence of shapes or objects and find the missing figure in the matrix
Bubble the right option
A or B or C or D

Lets Start the Test...

©All rights reserved-Math-Knots LLC., VA-USA

www.math-knots.com

©All rights reserved-Math-Knots LLC., VA-USA

www.math-knots.com

1)

(A) ○   (B) ○   (C) ○   (D) ○

2)

(A) ○   (B) ○   (C) ○   (D) ○

©All rights reserved-Math-Knots LLC., VA-USA
For more practice visit www.a4ace.com

3)

(A) ○   (B) ○   (C) ○   (D) ○

4)

(A) ○   (B) ○   (C) ○   (D) ○

©All rights reserved-Math-Knots LLC., VA-USA
For more practice visit www.a4ace.com

5)

(A) ○   (B) ○   (C) ○   (D) ○

6)

(A) ○   (B) ○   (C) ○   (D) ○

©All rights reserved-Math-Knots LLC., VA-USA
For more practice visit www.a4ace.com

www.math-knots.com

7)

(A) ○   (B) ○   (C) ○   (D) ○

8)

(A) ○   (B) ○   (C) ○   (D) ○

©All rights reserved-Math-Knots LLC., VA-USA
For more practice visit www.a4ace.com

www.math-knots.com

9)

(A) ○ (B) ○ (C) ○ (D) ○

10)

(A) ○ (B) ○ (C) ○ (D) ○

©All rights reserved-Math-Knots LLC., VA-USA
For more practice visit www.a4ace.com

www.math-knots.com

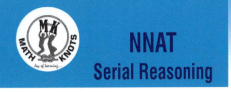
11)

(A)   (B)   (C)   (D)

12)

(A)   (B)   (C)   (D) ○

©All rights reserved-Math-Knots LLC., VA-USA
For more practice visit www.a4ace.com

www.math-knots.com

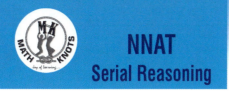
13)

(A)   (B)   (C)   (D)

14)

(A)   (B)   (C) ○   (D) ○

15)

(A) ○   (B) ○   (C) ○   (D) ○

TEST - 1

SPATIAL REASONING

Ask the students relate to each other and apply this relationship to the row with the empty frame. Visualize how the objects might look when flipped, rotated, transformed, or combined.

Lets Start the Test...

©All rights reserved-Math-Knots LLC., VA-USA

NNAT
Spatial Reasoning

1)

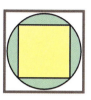 

(A) ○   (B) ○   (C) ○   (D) ○

2)

(A) ○   (B) ○   (C) ○   (D) ○

©All rights reserved-Math-Knots LLC., VA-USA
www.math-knots.com

3)

(A) ○ (B) ○ (C) ○ (D) ○

4)

(A) ○ (B) ○ (C) ○ (D) ○

©All rights reserved-Math-Knots LLC., VA-USA
www.math-knots.com

5)

(A) ○   (B) ○   (C) ○   (D) ○

6)

(A) ○   (B) ○   (C) ○   (D) ○

©All rights reserved-Math-Knots LLC., VA-USA

NNAT
Spatial Reasoning

GRADES : 4-5
Test 1

7)

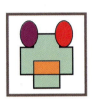

   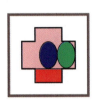

(A) ○   (B) ○   (C) ○   (D) ○

8)

(A) ○   (B) ○   (C) ○   (D) ○

©All rights reserved-Math-Knots LLC., VA-USA

9)

(A) ○   (B) ○   (C) ○   (D) ○

10)

(A) ○   (B) ○   (C) ○   (D) ○

©All rights reserved-Math-Knots LLC., VA-USA

www.math-knots.com

11)

(A) ○   (B) ○   (C) ○   (D) ○

12)

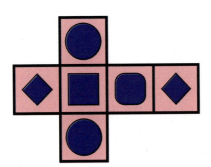

(A) ○   (B) ○   (C) ○   (D) ○

©All rights reserved-Math-Knots LLC., VA-USA

www.math-knots.com

13)

(A) ○   (B) ○   (C) ○   (D) ○

14)

(A) ○   (B) ○   (C) ○   (D) ○

©All rights reserved-Math-Knots LLC., VA-USA

www.math-knots.com

15)

(A)○   (B)○   (C)○   (D)○

16)

(A)○   (B)○   (C)○   (D)○

17)

(A) ○   (B) ○   (C) ○   (D) ○

18)

(A) ○   (B) ○   (C) ○   (D) ○

©All rights reserved-Math-Knots LLC., VA-USA
www.math-knots.com

19)

 ?

(A) ○   (B) ○   (C) ○   (D) ○

20)

 ?

(A) ○   (B) ○   (C) ○   (D) ○

©All rights reserved-Math-Knots LLC., VA-USA

www.math-knots.com

21)

(A) ○   (B) ○   (C) ○   (D) ○

22)

(A) ○   (B) ○   (C) ○   (D) ○

©All rights reserved-Math-Knots LLC., VA-USA

www.math-knots.com

23)

(A) ○   (B) ○   (C) ○   (D) ○

24)

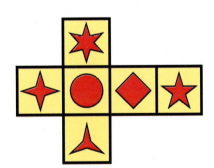

(A) ○   (B) ○   (C) ○   (D) ○

©All rights reserved-Math-Knots LLC., VA-USA
www.math-knots.com

25)

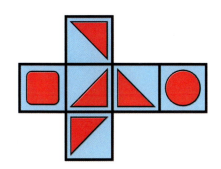

(A) ○

(B) ○

(C) ○

(D) ○

©All rights reserved-Math-Knots LLC., VA-USA

www.math-knots.com

©All rights reserved-Math-Knots LLC., VA-USA

www.math-knots.com

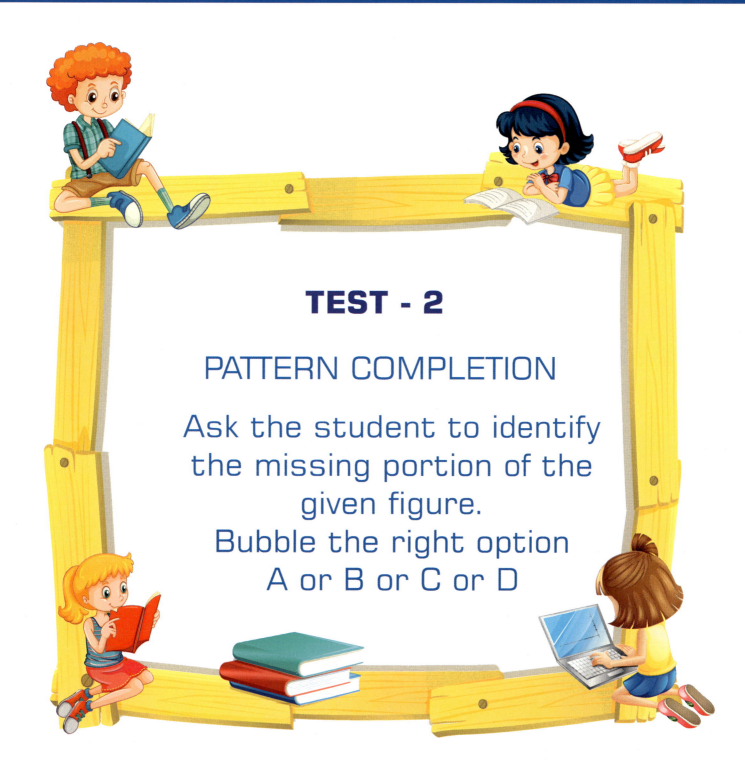

TEST - 2

PATTERN COMPLETION

Ask the student to identify the missing portion of the given figure.
Bubble the right option
A or B or C or D

Lets Start the Test...

©All rights reserved-Math-Knots LLC., VA-USA

www.math-knots.com

1)

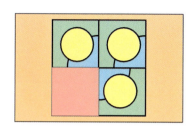

(A) ○   (B) ○   (C) ○   (D) ○

2)

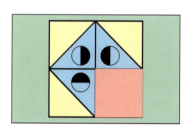

(A) ○   (B) ○   (C) ○   (D) ○

3)

(A) ○

(B) ○

(C) ○

(D) ○

4)

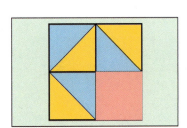

(A) ○

(B) ○

(C) ○

(D) ○

©All rights reserved-Math-Knots LLC., VA-USA
For more practice visit www.a4ace.com

5)

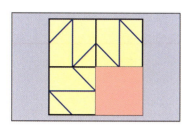

(A) ○   (B) ○   (C) ○   (D) ○

6)

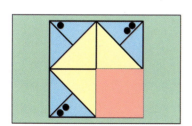

(A) ○   (B) ○   (C) ○   (D) ○

©All rights reserved-Math-Knots LLC., VA-USA
For more practice visit www.a4ace.com

www.math-knots.com

7)

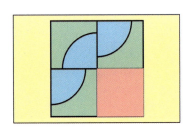

(A) ◯

(B) ◯

(C) ◯

(D) ◯

8)

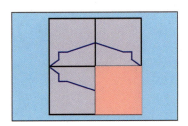

(A) ◯

(B) ◯

(C) ◯

(D) ◯

©All rights reserved-Math-Knots LLC., VA-USA
For more practice visit www.a4ace.com

9)

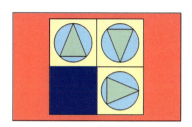

(A) ○

(B) ○

(C) ○

(D) ○

10)

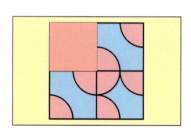

(A) ○

(B) ○

(C) ○

(D) ○

©All rights reserved-Math-Knots LLC., VA-USA
For more practice visit www.a4ace.com

www.math-knots.com

11)

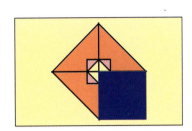

(A) ○

(B) ○

(C) ○

(D) ○

12)

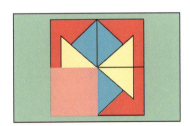

(A) ○

(B) ○

(C) ○

(D) ○

©All rights reserved-Math-Knots LLC., VA-USA
For more practice visit www.a4ace.com

9)

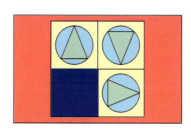

(A) ○

(B) ○

(C) ○

(D) ○

10)

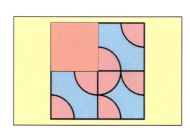

(A) ○

(B) ○

(C) ○

(D) ○

11)

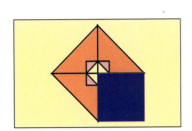

(A) ○

(B) ○

(C) ○

(D) ○

12)

(A) ○

(B) ○

(C) ○

(D) ○

©All rights reserved-Math-Knots LLC., VA-USA
For more practice visit www.a4ace.com

www.math-knots.com

13)

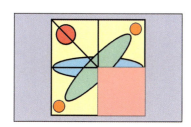

(A) ○

(B) ○

(C) ○

(D) ○

14)

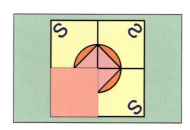

(A) ○

(B) ○

(C) ○

(D) ○

©All rights reserved-Math-Knots LLC., VA-USA
For more practice visit www.a4ace.com

www.math-knots.com

15)

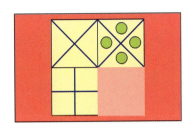

(A) ○

(B) ○

(C) ○

(D) ○

TEST - 2

REASON BY ANALOGY

Ask the student to identify the relationship between the abstract geometric shapes given in the first row based on the same relationship identify the missing figure in the second row. Bubble the right option A or B or C or D

Lets Start the Test...

©All rights reserved-Math-Knots LLC., VA-USA

www.math-knots.com

©All rights reserved-Math-Knots LLC., VA-USA

1)

(A) ○   (B) ○   (C) ○   (D) ○

2)

(A) ○   (B) ○   (C) ○   (D) ○

©All rights reserved-Math-Knots LLC., VA-USA

www.math-knots.com

3)

(A) ○   (B) ○   (C) ○   (D) ○

4)

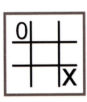 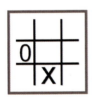

   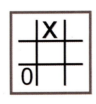

(A) ○   (B) ○   (C) ○   (D) ○

©All rights reserved-Math-Knots LLC., VA-USA
www.math-knots.com

5)

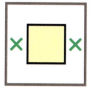

(A) ○ (B) ○ (C) ○ (D) ○

6)

(A) ○ (B) ○ (C) ○ (D) ○

©All rights reserved-Math-Knots LLC., VA-USA
www.math-knots.com

7)

(A) ○   (B) ○   (C) ○   (D) ○

8)

 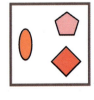 

(A) ○   (B) ○   (C) ○   (D) ○

©All rights reserved-Math-Knots LLC., VA-USA

www.math-knots.com

9)

(A) ○   (B) ○   (C) ○   (D) ○

10)

(A) ○   (B) ○   (C) ○   (D) ○

©All rights reserved-Math-Knots LLC., VA-USA
www.math-knots.com

11)

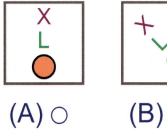

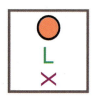

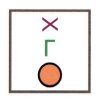

(A) ○   (B) ○   (C) ○   (D) ○

12)

(A) ○   (B) ○   (C) ○   (D) ○

©All rights reserved-Math-Knots LLC., VA-USA

www.math-knots.com

13)

   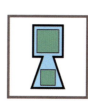

(A) ○   (B) ○   (C) ○   (D) ○

14)

 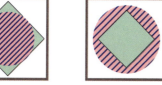 

(A) ○   (B) ○   (C) ○   (D) ○

©All rights reserved-Math-Knots LLC., VA-USA

www.math-knots.com

15)

 (A)○ (B)○ (C)○ (D)○

©All rights reserved-Math-Knots LLC., VA-USA

www.math-knots.com

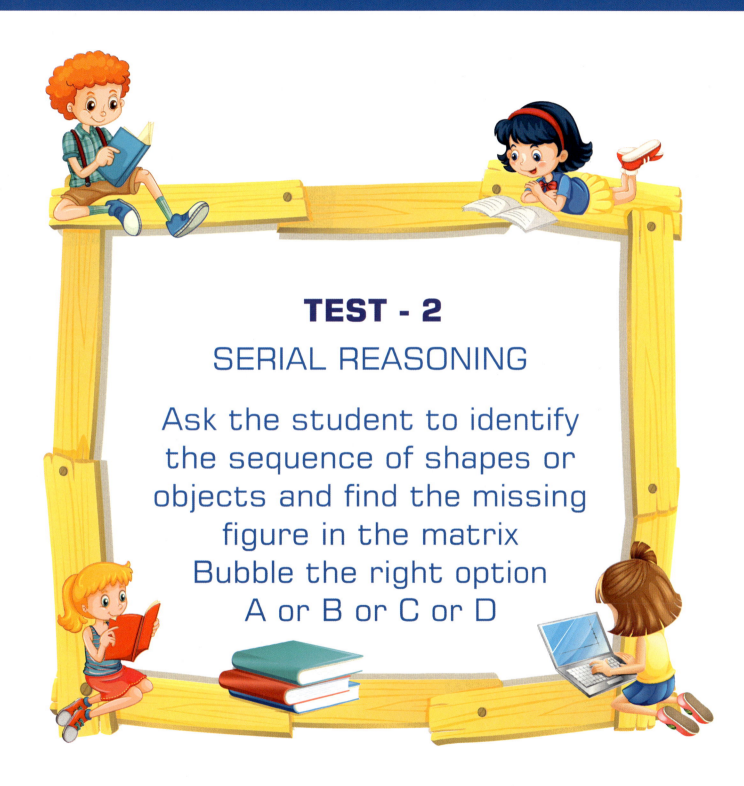

TEST - 2

SERIAL REASONING

Ask the student to identify the sequence of shapes or objects and find the missing figure in the matrix
Bubble the right option
A or B or C or D

Lets Start the Test...

©All rights reserved-Math-Knots LLC., VA-USA

www.math-knots.com

©All rights reserved-Math-Knots LLC., VA-USA

www.math-knots.com

1)

(A) ○   (B) ○   (C) ○   (D) ○

2)

(A) ○   (B) ○   (C) ○   (D) ○

3)

 (A) ○   (B) ○   (C) ○   (D) ○

4)

 (A) ○   (B) ○   (C) ○   (D) ○

©All rights reserved-Math-Knots LLC., VA-USA
For more practice visit a4ace.com

www.math-knots.com

5)

(A) ○   (B) ○   (C) ○   (D) ○

6)

(A) ○   (B) ○   (C) ○   (D) ○

©All rights reserved-Math-Knots LLC., VA-USA
For more practice visit a4ace.com

www.math-knots.com

7)

(A) ○   (B) ○   (C) ○   (D) ○

8)

(A) ○   (B) ○   (C) ○   (D) ○

©All rights reserved-Math-Knots LLC., VA-USA
For more practice visit a4ace.com

www.math-knots.com

5)

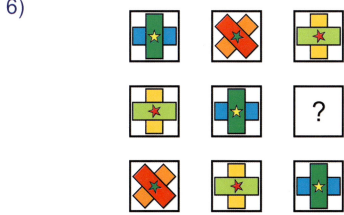

(A) ○   (B) ○   (C) ○   (D) ○

6)

(A) ○   (B) ○   (C) ○   (D) ○

©All rights reserved-Math-Knots LLC., VA-USA
For more practice visit a4ace.com
83
www.math-knots.com

7)

(A) ○ (B) ○ (C) ○ (D) ○

8)

(A) ○ (B) ○ (C) ○ (D) ○

©All rights reserved-Math-Knots LLC., VA-USA
For more practice visit a4ace.com

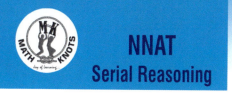
9)

 (A) ○ (B) ○ (C) ○ (D) ○

10)

 (A) ○ (B) ○ (C) ○ (D) ○

©All rights reserved-Math-Knots LLC., VA-USA
For more practice visit a4ace.com

www.math-knots.com

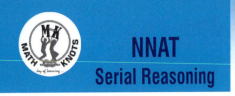
11)

(A) ○ 　(B) ○ 　(C) ○ 　(D) ○

12)

(A) ○ 　(B) ○ 　(C) ○ 　(D) ○

©All rights reserved-Math-Knots LLC., VA-USA
For more practice visit a4ace.com

www.math-knots.com

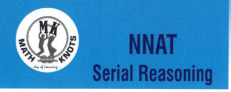

13)

(A) ○   (B) ○   (C) ○   (D) ○

14)

(A) ○   (B) ○   (C) ○   (D) ○

©All rights reserved-Math-Knots LLC., VA-USA
For more practice visit a4ace.com   87   www.math-knots.com

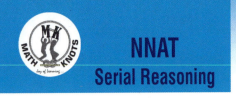

15)

(A) ○   (B) ○   (C) ○   (D) ○

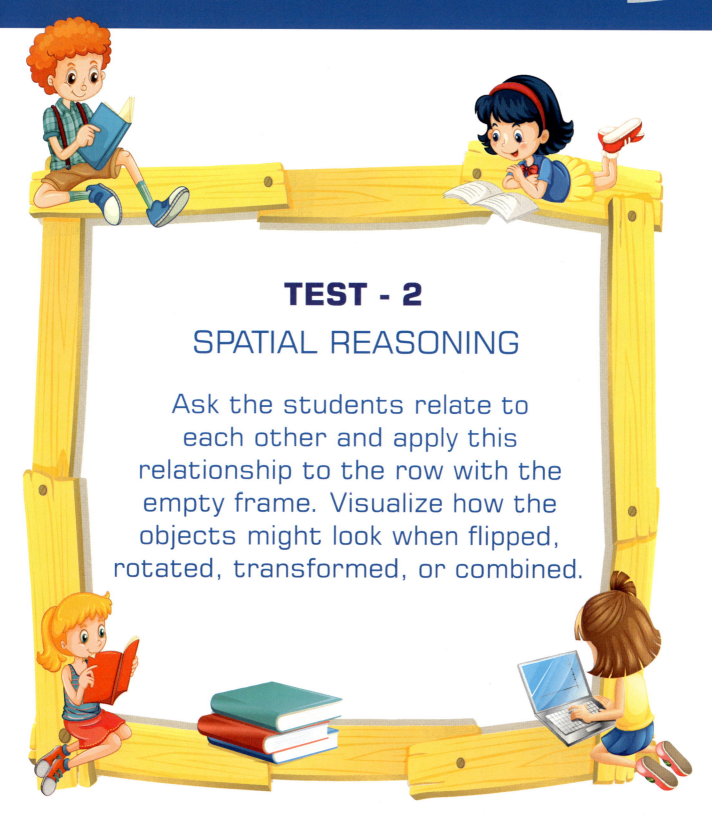

TEST - 2

SPATIAL REASONING

Ask the students relate to each other and apply this relationship to the row with the empty frame. Visualize how the objects might look when flipped, rotated, transformed, or combined.

Lets Start the Test...

©All rights reserved-Math-Knots LLC., VA-USA

www.math-knots.com

©All rights reserved-Math-Knots LLC., VA-USA

1)

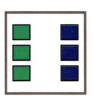 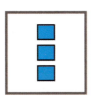

(A) ○　　　(B) ○　　　(C) ○　　　(D) ○

2)

(A) ○　　　(B) ○　　　(C) ○　　　(D) ○

©All rights reserved-Math-Knots LLC., VA-USA
www.math-knots.com

3)

(A) ○   (B) ○   (C) ○   (D) ○

4)

(A) ○   (B) ○   (C) ○   (D) ○

©All rights reserved-Math-Knots LLC., VA-USA

www.math-knots.com

5)

 ?

(A) ○   (B) ○   (C) ○   (D) ○

6)

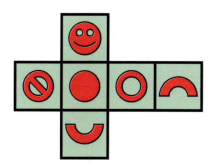

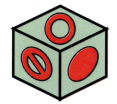   

(A) ○   (B) ○   (C) ○   (D) ○

©All rights reserved-Math-Knots LLC., VA-USA
www.math-knots.com

7)

(A) ○   (B) ○   (C) ○   (D) ○

8)

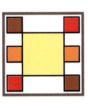

(A) ○   (B) ○   (C) ○   (D) ○

©All rights reserved-Math-Knots LLC., VA-USA
www.math-knots.com

9)

(A) ○　　　(B) ○　　　(C) ○　　　(D) ○

10)

(A) ○　　　(B) ○　　　(C) ○　　　(D) ○

©All rights reserved-Math-Knots LLC., VA-USA　　　95

11)

   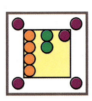

(A) ○   (B) ○   (C) ○   (D) ○

12)

(A) ○   (B) ○   (C) ○   (D) ○

©All rights reserved-Math-Knots LLC., VA-USA

www.math-knots.com

9)

(A) ○   (B) ○   (C) ○   (D) ○

10)

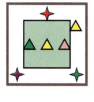   

(A) ○   (B) ○   (C) ○   (D) ○

©All rights reserved-Math-Knots LLC., VA-USA
www.math-knots.com

11)

   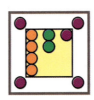

(A) ○   (B) ○   (C) ○   (D) ○

12)

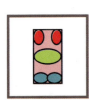

(A) ○   (B) ○   (C) ○   (D) ○

©All rights reserved-Math-Knots LLC., VA-USA
www.math-knots.com

13)

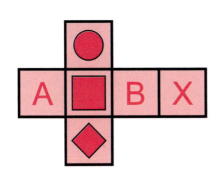

(A) ○   (B) ○   (C) ○   (D) ○

14)

  ?

 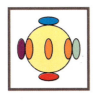  

(A) ○   (B) ○   (C) ○   (D) ○

©All rights reserved-Math-Knots LLC., VA-USA
www.math-knots.com

15)

(A) ○   (B) ○   (C) ○   (D) ○

16)

(A) ○   (B) ○   (C) ○   (D) ○

©All rights reserved-Math-Knots LLC., VA-USA
www.math-knots.com

17)

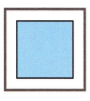

(A) ○   (B) ○   (C) ○   (D) ○

18)

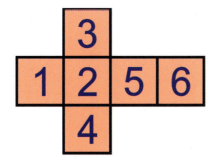

(A) ○   (B) ○   (C) ○   (D) ○

©All rights reserved-Math-Knots LLC., VA-USA   www.math-knots.com

19)

(A) ○   (B) ○   (C) ○   (D) ○

20)

(A) ○   (B) ○   (C) ○   (D) ○

21)

   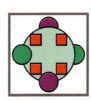

(A) ○   (B) ○   (C) ○   (D) ○

22)

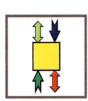

(A) ○   (B) ○   (C) ○   (D) ○

©All rights reserved-Math-Knots LLC., VA-USA
www.math-knots.com

23)

(A) ○   (B) ○   (C) ○   (D) ○

24)

(A) ○   (B) ○   (C) ○   (D) ○

©All rights reserved-Math-Knots LLC., VA-USA

www.math-knots.com

25)

(A) ○   (B) ○   (C) ○   (D) ○

©All rights reserved-Math-Knots LLC., VA-USA

www.math-knots.com

©All rights reserved-Math-Knots LLC., VA-USA

www.math-knots.com

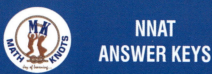

TEST 1 - 2

ANSWER KEYS

Lets Start the Test...

©All rights reserved-Math-Knots LLC., VA-USA

www.math-knots.com

©All rights reserved-Math-Knots LLC., VA-USA

www.math-knots.com

Test 1		Test 2	
1.	A	1.	D
2.	B	2.	B
3.	D	3.	C
4.	B	4.	D
5.	A	5.	C
6.	C	6.	C
7.	D	7.	A
8.	B	8.	C
9.	C	9.	A
10.	A	10.	B
11.	A	11.	C
12.	B	12.	C
13.	A	13.	D
14.	A	14.	C
15.	A	15.	D

©All rights reserved-Math-Knots LLC., VA-USA
www.math-knots.com

Test 1		Test 2	
1.	A	1.	A
2.	C	2.	C
3.	D	3.	B
4.	A	4.	D
5.	C	5.	A
6.	B	6.	A
7.	B	7.	B
8.	A	8.	C
9.	A	9.	B
10.	B	10.	C
11.	D	11.	D
12.	A	12.	A
13.	C	13.	B
14.	C	14.	C
15.	B	15.	A

Test 1		Test 2	
1.	C	1.	C
2.	A	2.	B
3.	D	3.	D
4.	A	4.	C
5.	B	5.	A
6.	A	6.	A
7.	B	7.	B
8.	C	8.	C
9.	A	9.	C
10.	B	10.	A
11.	C	11.	A
12.	D	12.	D
13.	C	13.	B
14.	A	14.	A
15.	B	15.	A

©All rights reserved-Math-Knots LLC., VA-USA
www.math-knots.com

NNAT
Spatial Reasoning

GRADES : 4-5
Answer Keys

Test 1

1.	A	17.	A
2.	D	18.	C
3.	A	19.	B
4.	C	20.	D
5.	A	21.	B
6.	C	22.	D
7.	B	23.	A
8.	D	24.	B
9.	C	25.	A
10.	A		
11.	C		
12.	C		
13.	A		
14.	D		
15.	C		
16.	C		

Test 2

1.	A	17.	A
2.	D	18.	D
3.	A	19.	A
4.	C	20.	C
5.	A	21.	B
6.	C	22.	D
7.	B	23.	B
8.	D	24.	D
9.	A	25.	A
10.	D		
11.	C		
12.	A		
13.	A		
14.	A		
15.	A		
16.	D		

©All rights reserved-Math-Knots LLC., VA-USA

www.math-knots.com

Made in the USA
Columbia, SC
29 January 2022

55016412R00062